D0572614

FORCES OF NATURE
Floods

By S.L. Hamilton

Visit us at
www.abdopublishing.com

Published by ABDO Publishing Company, PO Box 398166, Minneapolis, MN 55439. Copyright ©2012 by Abdo Consulting Group, Inc. International copyrights reserved in all countries. No part of this book may be reproduced in any form without written permission from the publisher. A&D Xtreme™ is a trademark and logo of ABDO Publishing Company.

Printed in the United States of America, North Mankato, Minnesota.
102011
012012

 PRINTED ON RECYCLED PAPER

Editor: John Hamilton
Graphic Design: Sue Hamilton
Cover Design: John Hamilton
Cover Photo: Getty
Interior Photos: AP-pgs 4-7, 14-23, 28-29, & 32; Corbis-pgs 10-11, 24-25, 26-27, & 30-31; Getty Images-pgs 1; John Hamilton-pgs 8-9; Library of Congress-pgs 12 & 13; NASA/GSFC Scientific Visualization Studio-pg 7; Thinkstock-pgs 2-3.

ABDO Booklinks
Web sites about Forces of Nature are featured on our Book Links pages. These links are routinely monitored and updated to provide the most current information available.
Web site: www.abdopublishing.com

Library of Congress Cataloging-in-Publication Data

Hamilton, Sue L., 1959-
  Floods / S.L. Hamilton.
       p. cm. -- (Forces of nature)
  Includes index.
  ISBN 978-1-61783-260-4
  1. Floods--Juvenile literature. I. Title.
  GB1399.H36 2012
  551.48'9--dc23
                        2011029871

Contents

Raging Water!

A flood occurs when water covers land that is usually dry. When billions of gallons of raging, muddy, debris-filled water blasts into people, buildings, and land, it's a terrifying, unstoppable force of nature.

XTREME FACT – As little as six inches of fast-moving floodwater is enough to knock someone off their feet.

The Science

Flooding occurs when extreme weather brings more water than the ground or rivers, lakes, and streams can absorb. Heavy rainfall, fast snowmelt, or even tropical storms or hurricanes moving inland can bring huge amounts of water. Sometimes, a broken dam can cause catastrophic flooding.

Floodwaters from the Missouri River surround a home in 1993.

Above: *A NASA image of a section of the Missouri River in 1992.*
Below: *The same area in September 1993, showing flooding.*

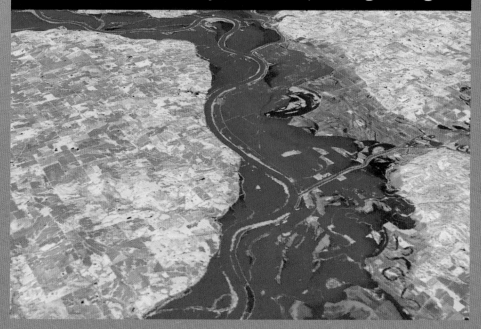

Flash Floods

Many floods occur slowly, with steadily rising water over a period of days. A flash flood develops in a matter of minutes or hours. Caused by heavy rainfall, such as by a stalled thunderstorm, the water blasts down creek beds or asphalt-covered roads. It can tear up the ground, roll boulders, rip out trees, and carry away bridges.

XTREME FACT – In a flash flood, it may take less than a minute for a creek bed to go from bone dry to a raging torrent with great walls of water 10-20 feet (3-6 m) high.

A flash flood moves through Coalpits Wash, near Zion National Park, Utah. Moments earlier, the area was nearly dry.

Inland Floods

Extreme weather conditions such as tropical cyclones and hurricanes often move over land. These storms may drop incredible amounts of rain, causing dangerous inland flooding.

A North Carolina community was severely flooded when Hurricane Irene moved inland in 2011.

XTREME FACT – *A car, even a bus, can be carried off by as little as two feet (.6 m) of floodwater.*

Historic Floods

Any place on Earth where rain falls is at risk for flooding. Some floods have been so devastating they will always be remembered.

After days of heavy rain, Pennsylvania's South Fork Dam collapsed on May 31, 1889. The city of Johnstown sat 14 miles (23 km) away, directly in the path of the raging torrent. Floodwaters blasted the town, destroying most of the buildings and killing 2,200 people. This is still one of the worst disasters in United States history.

People sort through the debris that was once their town.

Downtown Dayton, Ohio, in the spring of 1913.

The Flood of 1913 became known as "Ohio's greatest weather disaster." Heavy March rains flooded many parts of the state, killing 467 people and destroying 40,000 homes.

The Ohio River Flood of 1937 hit parts of Ohio, Kentucky, Indiana, and Illinois. Heavy rains in January and February caused flooding in more than 12,700 square miles (32,893 sq km) of land, leaving 600,000 people without homes.

Floodwaters rise in the streets of Louisville, Kentucky.

Infamous Floods

Lowlands bordering water, such as rivers and oceans, are called floodplains. They may flood each year. However, in certain years, extreme amounts of water can cause unexpected, catastrophic damage.

North Dakota-2011

In the spring and summer of 2011, North Dakota faced severe flooding from the Missouri and Souris Rivers. Massive rainstorms in Canada, along with fast snowmelt, brought floodwaters that surrounded and, in some cases, washed away homes and businesses.

A home breaks apart in June 2011 as it is engulfed by Missouri River floodwaters near Bismarck, North Dakota.

XTREME FACT – Since 1900, floods have killed more than 10,000 people in the United States alone.

Tennessee-2010

XTREME FACT – A 1,000-year flood is a flood that has a .1 percent chance of occurring. This flood level happens on average only once every 1,000 years.

In May 2010, Tennessee experienced a 1,000-year flood. On May 1-2, storms brought 19 inches (48 cm) of rain to parts of the state, causing massive flooding and 21 deaths.

An Elvis Presley statue sits on the flooded porch of a Nashville, Tennessee, restaurant in May 2010. The Cumberland River, which runs through the center of Nashville, swelled over its banks, flooding many areas of the city.

Mid-Atlantic-2006

In June 2006, heavy rains brought extreme flooding to the Mid-Atlantic region of the United States. People in the states of New York, Pennsylvania, New Jersey, Maryland, Delaware, Virginia, and Washington, D.C., faced washed out roads, destroyed homes, and damaged businesses. Sixteen people lost their lives in one of the area's worst floods in more than 25 years.

A National Guardsman is lowered by helicopter to rescue a man whose tractor was washed off a flooded road in Pennsylvania in June 2006.

XTREME FACT – Sixty-six percent of flood deaths are in vehicles. Drivers make the tragic mistake of trying to cross flooded roads and are swept away.

New Orleans-2005

XTREME QUOTE – "In the last 30 years, inland flooding has been responsible for more than half the deaths associated with tropical cyclones in the United States." ~Ed Rappaport, National Hurricane Center

New Orleans faced severe flooding when Hurricane Katrina came ashore in August 2005. The storm brought so much rain that water surged over the top of many of the city's levees. In addition, several of New Orleans' floodwalls broke. Much of the city was flooded. In human lives and destruction, this was one of the costliest natural disasters in the United States.

A man pushes his bicycle through flood waters near the Superdome in New Orleans in August 2005. People were told to leave, but many ignored warnings and stayed. More than 1,500 people died.

Houston-2001

In June 2001, Houston, Texas, stood in the path of Tropical Storm Allison. The city received 40 inches (102 cm) of rain, causing massive flooding. Twenty people died, and the flooding cost billions of dollars in damages.

10 WES
QUITMAN S
LEFT EXIT

XTREME FACT – One-third of flooded roads and bridges are so damaged by water that any vehicle trying to cross stands only a 50 percent chance of making it to the other side.

EXIT 48A

🛡 10 EAST

Beaumont

EXIT ⬇ ONLY

48A
10 EAST
Beaumont

EXIT 48B

🛡 10 WEST

San Antonio

EXIT ⬇ ONLY

EXIT 49B

WEST
EXIT 49A

Quitman St ↗

Streets and highways were flooded, stopping traffic and shutting down parts of Houston in June 2001.

Red River Flood-1997

In early April 1997, warm temperatures in North Dakota quickly melted the great snowfall of the season, causing the Red River to rise rapidly. Cresting at 54 feet (16 m), floodwaters reached 3 miles (5 km) inland. More than 50,000 people were evacuated from the town of Grand Forks, North Dakota. In the United States, this was one of the largest group of people ever to be displaced from their homes. The Red River also flooded parts of Canada, South Dakota, and Minnesota. Damages grew to $5 billion dollars.

A flooded Grand Forks, North Dakota, in 1997.

In North Dakota, a rescuer checks flooded homes near the Red River in April 1997.

Great Flood of 1993

The Great Flood of 1993 happened when both the Missouri and Mississippi Rivers flooded 400,000 square miles (1,035,995 sq km) in parts of 9 Midwestern states. Fifty people died, more than 50,000 homes were damaged, and 12,000 miles of farmland were washed out. The Great Flood lasted for an unbelievable 200 days in certain areas, and caused $15 billion in damage.

In August 1993, Missouri River floodwaters swamped an airport in Chesterfield, Missouri.

A humorous sign acknowledges the Mississippi River's severe flooding in July 1993.

Surviving a Flood

Being prepared and informed is the best way to survive a flood. Prepare a disaster kit that includes enough food and bottled water for three days for each person. If officials tell you to leave, do so immediately. Do NOT cross flooded roads. If trapped in a building, move to the highest area. Bring a radio or other device and listen to official updates.

XTREME FACT – The American Red Cross recommends having a gallon of drinking water per person per day in disaster kits.

People await rescue on a roof after floodwaters rose in New Orleans in 2005.

Glossary

CATASTROPHIC
Great danger that is often sudden or unexpected, which typically leads to great losses of life and property.

EVACUATE
To leave a dangerous place to go to a place of safety.

FLASH FLOOD
A sudden, often unexpected flood that occurs because of heavy rains in a specific location.

FLOODPLAIN
A low-lying area next to a body of water, such as a river, that is frequently covered with floodwater.

FLOODWALL
A man-made wall designed to hold back floodwater from an area. See also Levee.

HURRICANE
A violent storm with wind speeds greater than 74 miles per hour (119 kph) and heavy rains.

INLAND FLOODING
Flooding that occurs when an unusual amount of heavy rain occurs in a specific area. This often happens when a tropical storm or hurricane comes ashore.

LEVEE
An earthen or stone wall built beside a river and designed to hold back floodwater. See also Floodwall.

RED CROSS
An organization that cares for people who have been hurt or left homeless due to war or natural disasters, such as flood victims.

TROPICAL CYCLONE
A violent, rotating storm that forms over warm waters. It is more commonly known as a hurricane or tropical storm, and is characterized by high winds and heavy rain.

Index

In North Dakota, a dog looks at her flooded yard after the Red River swelled over its banks again in 2009.